The
Discipline
Of Raising Children

By
M. A. Treadwell, M.D.

THE DISCIPLINE OF RAISING
CHILDREN
Copyright © 1977 Harvest House Publishers
Irvine, California 92714
Library of Congress Catalog Number:
77-71214
ISBN 0-89081-040-0
Printed in the United States of America

PREFACE

With all the fine books already published on parenting, why another one? It is not very long; it does not go into great detail. It does not give the latest theories and discuss the pros and cons of various well-known schools of thought.

Instead, I wrote this kind of book because I think there are many parents who are looking for some help that is simple, briefly stated, and right to the point. Some readers may find me a bit too simplistic, a bit too authoritarian, and even a bit naive. They may say, "It just isn't that easy."

I am well aware—after 26 years of medical practice and rearing three children of my own—that there are certain basics that parents must consider. As I have worked with my patients—both children and their parents—I have become increasingly aware that many families are not operating on a solid foundation of basic principles that can bring them success.

In these brief pages, I try to give you some of those principles. There is much I don't say, but I'm more interested in having you *consider carefully* what I do say. I know it can be done, because my wife and I did it with our own three children. All of them achieved excellent records in high school and college. One son is a surgeon, another is in medical school. Our daughter is happily married to a medical resident at Baylor Hospital in Dallas, Texas. All three are active, dedicated Christians.

I don't write from some ivory tower, looking down on all the parents who have problems, who are unsure of which way to turn. My wife and I have known our share of problems; we made our share of mistakes. But we also did some things right, and I want to share these ideas with you.

You may not find anything here that is new and "revolutionary," but you will find practical, usable principles based directly on the Bible. Parents who will commit themselves completely to practicing these concepts have God's word on it. . .they will raise children they can be proud of!

M. A. Treadwell, M.D.

CONTENTS

1

What It's All About

Parenthood brings to mind the matter of the birds and bees; or more properly, in this age of overemphasis on sex, the matter of the ova and the sperm. Unfortunately, becoming parents requires no intelligence, no talents, no love of, or desire for, children. In fact, many parents are parents only as a by-product of the satisfaction of certain biological urges. Adopted children are fortunate in that they know their parents *wanted* to be parents. Not all children have this assurance.

Good parents start planning and preparing even before the first child arrives. Good parents look forward anxiously to the coming of the baby and make all arrangements for clothing, bed, food, etc. for the new arrival. During these months of preparation, the "parents to be" are subjected to all kinds of advice, warnings, age-old superstitions, and "old wives tales." The only safe course is to ignore any advice not given by your doctor.

Finally, the long awaited day arrives, and you are parents. You are filled with the wonder and thrill of that first boy or girl, so sweet, so tiny, so dependent. With mixed feelings of anxiety, fear, and determination, the true task of parenthood begins. Many good books on child rearing are available, and your doctor is willing to advise and help with the care of the child. But beware of "helpful" friends, for they tend to confuse with their misinformation and superstitions.

PERMISSIVENESS DOESN'T WORK

Different methods of rearing children emerge from time to time. Our nation has swung from the rigid discipline era to the permissive era; hence, we are now suffering from a generation of disrespectful, immoral, inconsiderate, confused young people who were reared in a climate of parental permissiveness. These "kinds" were never corrected, never punished, never made to respect their parents. As a result they have no respect for any authority be it home, school, or civil. In the years of rigid and strict family discipline, a discipline usually administered by the father, children were to be seen and not heard. The parent's word was law, and strict obedience was demanded. This type of discipline was much better for the world than the permissive era, but certainly a mixture of these two concepts of rearing children is more ideal.

My goal in this book is to help parents *who want to have successful, happy children.* I hope to give you practical, proven ideas for nurturing your children in such a way that they will eventually be happy, mature individuals. To accomplish this you must be willing to spend a great deal of time with your children. This usually means that you will have to give up many outside activities with friends in order to be with your children. Most of your recreation and relaxation will be with the family as you teach and guide each child. Frequently, you will have to stand alone, because some of your friends will let their children do things that you disagree with or know are not best. As parents you must not just instruct and teach the children; you must live your teachings each day. Setting a good example is much more impressive to your children than just telling them what to do. In fact, no amount of teaching will convince a child of something if your example is contrary to your words.

"Your actions speak so loudly I can't hear a word you say," is certainly true for parents. Good manners are taught *by* example much more easily than by instruction *without* example.

Even though parenthood is a full time job, it does not mean that the parents must neglect one another. An essential part of a child's development is seeing and feeling the relationship of love in the home. The constant atmosphere of love created by affection shown and spoken by husband to wife, wife to husband, and by both parents to the child gives him a sense of security. It gives him a feeling of closeness to his parents, and prepares him for proper relationships of love in his own family in later years.

PARENTS MUST SET GOALS

All parental teaching and guidance must be toward a goal. As early as possible in life, you should help your child set goals and then work together to reach them. During earlier years a basic goal for every child is to do the best he is capable of doing in each thing he undertakes—studies, athletics, hobbies, etc. For example, before my children started grade school, each child knew about college and graduate school, each child knew his goal (or goals) included college and preparation for a career. I am not suggesting, of course, that parents should select their child's life's work. What is vitally important, however, is instilling in the child the desire for accomplishment and encouraging the child in the field in which he shows interest and talents.

Parents must also show the child the joy

and value of a happy home and a successful marriage. But even early in life, parents should emphasize that marriage follows educational plans. All the while parents should be pointing the child toward the final goal of a full and happy life as a mature adult doing a job that is satisfying and worthwhile.

My interest in child development comes from several sources. First, when I was a child, I realized that very few of my playmates and friends had the love and attention that I received from my parents. And as my contemporaries and I grew older, they lacked the happiness and self-assurance that I had. Second, I gained a great deal of experience as my wife and I reared our three children, Terry, Marsha and Randall.

Third, as I received my medical education, I was aware that not nearly enough emphasis was placed on helping children develop properly. Fourth, as a Christian, I read in the Bible the many, many instructions about rearing children and realized how few parents carried out these instructions given by the expert of experts, our Maker. Some of these instructions are given in the following scripture passages.

"And all thy children shall be taught of the Lord; and great shall be the peace of thy children" (Is. 54:13, KJV).

"Train up a child in the way he should go: and when he is old, he will not depart from it" (Prov. 22:6, KJV).

"Foolishness is bound in the heart of a child, but the rod of correction shall drive it far from him" (Prov. 22:15, KJV).

"A wise son heareth his father's instruction..." (Prov. 13:1, KJV).

And now a word to you parents. Don't keep on scolding and nagging your children, making them angry and resentful. Rather, bring them up with the loving discipline the Lord himself approves, with suggestions and godly advice" (Eph. 6:4, TLB).

"If you refuse to discipline your son, it proves you don't love him; for if

you love him you will be prompt to punish him" (Prov. 13:24, TLB). (Living Bible)

"Correct thy son, and he shall give thee rest; yea, he shall give delight unto thy soul" (Prov. 29:17, KJV).

In the following pages, I will attempt to guide you, an interested, concerned parent, through the many phases of a child's development. I will point out some of the problems that may arise at each phase and how best to handle these problems in order to arrive at the goal of "a child you'll be proud to admit is your own."

2

Infancy:
The Important Beginning

The period of development from birth to age two years is usually called the infancy stage. This is a most important stage, because the habits established by the parents during this time will frequently determine the future growth and development of the child. There are few real problems during infancy, but the proper handling of these problems is very important.

One of the first problems encountered is the new relationship between husband, wife, and baby. A tiny baby is sweet and wonderful, but actually he is not as much fun as an older child, especially for the father. For this reason, it is easy for the father to have very little to do with the baby, because he would actually prefer to wait until the child is older and more responsive before spending time with him.

The mother gets so busy caring for the new baby that the father feels left out. The mother may get so tired and so involved with baby's schedule that she does not give her husband the attention he is accustomed to and deserves. This leads to tensions and a sense of separation between husband and wife at a time when they should be drawn closer together than ever before by their mutual accomplishment, the new baby.

LET FATHER IN ON BABY'S CARE

These problems can be prevented by including father in the care of the baby. When he has time, father should help feed, bathe, clothe, and, yes, even change the baby! This will give the child assurance that he is loved by both parents and will make the father feel very much involved with the new arrival. Baby's schedule should be arranged so that the mother and father have some time together—without the baby—to enjoy each other. This is best accomplished by arranging the baby's achedule so that he has his last feeding by 6:00 P.M. and is immediately placed in his own bed for the night. For the first few weeks the baby will require a 10:00 P.M. and maybe a 2:00 A.M. feeding. At these times the baby is given a bottle (or nursed), burped, changed, and immediately put to bed.

I mention that the baby be put to sleep *in his own bed* for a purpose. There have been instances where parents have allowed a child to sleep with them in their bed for as long as three or four years. This is very foolish. In the first place, the baby sleeps much better alone in his own bed and is much safer. Babies have been smothered to death while sleeping with adults. Secondly, the mother and father will enjoy each other more and sleep more normally with the baby safely in his own bassinette or bed, preferably in another room.

HOW TO HANDLE TWO MAJOR PROBLEMS

Two main problems of infancy are feeding and behavior. How these problems are handled often determines who will run the family for years to come. If parents cannot conquer an infant, they can never expect to control an insolent, rebellious teenager.

Feeding should be established on a schedule. Some books recommend a so-called "self-demand" schedule, but the baby cannot tell you when he is hungry. (After many years in the business, I still cannot tell if a baby is hungry or if he is fussing from some other cause). The best plan for a normal, healthy baby is to establish a four-hour feeding schedule. (You may want to vary this 30 minutes either way in case the child is asleep, or if he is already awake and fretful). A consistent four-hour feeding schedule will usually insure against the baby getting overly hungry.

When the child is fed, he should be burped and immediately placed in his own bed and left alone. He will usually go to sleep. However, if baby wants to lie in the bed and play, let him. If he cries, check to be sure that a pin is not sticking him and that his diaper is not dirty; then let him cry. If the baby is not picked up, he will learn to sleep or play until his next feeding time.

HOW TO CURE "COLIC"

Babies, even tiny ones, are smart; they learn rapidly. If a baby cries and is picked up and walked or rocked, he learns about the third time he is picked up that he is to cry *until* he is picked up. This will usually satisfy baby at first, but it will not be long before he becomes uncomfortable as he is being held, and his crying begins anew. When placed back in his bed, the baby still cries because he has already learned to cry until he is picked up. An so begins the major calamity of the newborn, the "colic!!"

Of course, no grandmother and very few mothers will agree that "colic" is just a spoiled child, but it is usually so. "Colic" can be prevented or cured by feeding the baby on schedule, placing him in his bed, and, if necessary, letting him cry until he learns that he is to eat, then go to bed. He will learn this properly if parents, and especially grandparents, will let him. Certainly it is hard to let "the poor little thing" cry, unless you realize it is for his own good and that the cries stop when he is properly trained.

"Colic" is almost always confined to the first child in a family. The reason for this is that when the second and subsequent children arrive the parents are still so busy with the spoiled child that the next baby is "neglected" just enough so he is not picked up at every movement he makes. Hence, he is not taught to cry *until* he is picked up. Then, too, the parents are more at ease with a second child.

Rarely, of course, is there an organic cause for the "colic." If symptoms persist, the baby's doctor can rule out any medical problems such as milk allergies or some type of intestinal blockage.

WHEN BABY CRIES, BE FIRM!

Mother, father, grandparents, and even other children in the family have a hard time staying away from the baby when he cries. One of my patients said that she just could not stand to hear her baby cry, so she picked the baby up every time she made a noise. As a result the mother carried the infant almost the entire first year of her life! The mother insisted that carrying the child was easier than letting her infant daughter cry. Far too many children are spoiled in this manner, and the mother missed one of the first opportunities to discipline the youngster.

My wife learned the hard way on our first child. She had very little trouble with him during the day, but after his 6:00 P.M. feeding, he seemed to know that daddy would soon be home and different things would be happening. After the boy was put down for the night, he fretted, cried, and screamed. Because my wife "loved" the little fellow so much, she picked him up the first few nights, because she "just knew" there was something wrong with him. Even though I assured my wife that our infant son was fine and that she should leave him in bed to cry, she simply could not believe my advice. However, it finally dawned on her that our child was "ill" only after the 6:00 P.M. feeding. So after one more exhausting evening, my wife decided that she would try my advice.

My wife still vows that the next evening was one of the hardest she ever endured. She listened to her precious angel cry and cry; it was almost too much. Just as her nerves and her resolve were giving way (he cried for almost three hours) her little boy stopped crying and was soon sleeping peacefully and exhaustedly. The next evening the crying was of shorter duration; the third evening the crying did not occur. Her precious angel had learned his first lesson in discipline. As a result of this experience, our second and third children never had the "colic" at all.

During the day if baby wakes up, cries, and it is not yet feeding time, offer him water in a bottle and play with him. This is a much better time to play and enjoy the baby rather than right after his feeding when he is full and should go to bed and to sleep.

If properly worked out, the approximate four-hour schedule will get the baby to bed about 6:00 P.M., giving the parents a quiet, peaceful evening together. Of course, some mothers do not like starting the day at 6:00 A.M., but this is usually better than having the baby up until the parents' bedtime.

TIPS ON GETTING A CHILD TO EAT

As the child grows, other foods are added, and eventually three meals a day are scheduled. As foods are added, they should be fed by a spoon and not mixed with the formula. This way the baby learns the taste and consistency of each new food. Spoon feeding is messy and slow at first, but patience and persistence are usually rewarded by a "good eater." Remember that a child's appetite may vary. If he refuses foods just stop trying to get him to eat and wait until the next feeding time to offer more food. By then the child will be hungry and will eat. Never bribe or trick the child into eating.

One patient I knew was so determined to have her first child eat that she diverted his attention with all sorts of toys and noises as she poked spoonful after spoonful of food down the youngster. The boy did not know or care what he was eating; he was playing. When the lady's next two children reached this stage, she was too busy to trick them into eating. She only fed them what they were willing to eat at mealtime. To this mother's surprise her last two children were wonderful eaters while the first child was a problem eater for many years.

It is important for the child to understand that if he does not eat the food put before him at mealtime, he will get nothing to eat until the next regular feeding. However, if he eats well at mealtimes, he may have treats between meals.

As the child gets older, he quickly learns that one of the best ways to upset mother is not to eat. This will be no problem if the mother is firm, persistent, and does not give in and let the child eat anything between meals.

SOME BAD HABITS AND HOW TO AVOID THEM

Many times as the child gets older, the parents let him eat his food off his plate or tray with his hands. This is fine with crackers or cookies but should not be done with most foods. It does the child no good and results in a terrible mess. Food is spread all over the tray, the child, and the floor. The mother or dad should feed the baby with a spoon until the child is old enough to use the spoon himself without making too big a mess. Eating soft foods with one's hands is certainly not teaching the baby anything useful.

Another bad habit that some parents have is letting a bottle of milk, juice or (heaven forbid!!!) coke sit around the house all day so that the toddler can grab the bottle when he pleases. This creates a bad eating habit and often keeps the baby from eating well at mealtimes. Allowing the baby to take milk from a bottle too long slows him down on accepting new foods. Most babies should be taken off the bottle or breast somewhere between six to twelve months. As soon as the child can drink from a cup, it is a good idea to throw away the bottle and give milk from a cup. Usually less milk will be taken, but the child will eat more foods—cereal, fruits, vegetables, meats, etc. Anytime I see a baby that is old enough to walk carrying a bottle, I know someone is failing to teach this child properly.

Yet another bad habit of infancy is giving baby a bottle to suck on in bed. It is much wiser to hold the baby while giving the bottle; burp him and then put him to bed to sleep. It is frequently a help to give the baby a pacifier to suck on if he does not go to sleep promptly. Many infants will suck their thumbs or fingers, so a pacifier is much easier to throw away than a finger when the child is eighteen months to two years old.

The child's behavior is taught by word and example. Children learn by repetition, so instruction must be given over and over until the child understands what he is to do. This process of teaching begins in the new born. As I mentioned earlier, the crying baby has to be picked up only three or four times before he learns to cry *until* he is picked up.

The small child understands the word "no," and quickly learns what behavior gets praise and affection and what behavior gets disapproval and punishment. Some parents do not realize that the young child can understand, and they become guilty of allowing the child to do almost anything without punishment or even correction. This results in a child who grows up not knowing the meaning of discipline, and who has no respect for any authority, parental or otherwise.

PARENTS MUST BE CONSISTENT

As the child learns to crawl, stand and walk, patient, repetitious guidance must be applied in teaching him the many things he must know. The child must learn what things he can play with and what things he must leave alone. Even a small child will learn this if he is corrected *consistently*.

In all of our discipline, it is necessary to be consistent. If we say "no" one time and "yes" the next, the child becomes confused and never learns properly. Both mother and father must try to teach the same thing. If one parent is not consistent or if the parents do not agree on points of discipline, the young child is confused. And in later years he quickly learns to play one parent against the other and to take advantage of the lenient or inconsistent parent. Parents should settle their differences of opinion in private and agree on a course of action so that they will be in agreement when they correct or instruct the child.

3

The Toddler: Moving On

After the "colic" phase the infant is fairly easy to handle until a period from about eighteen months to two and a half years. At this stage the child is negativistic; he says "no" to everything and seems to enjoy doing just the opposite of what he is told or what he knows is expected of him.

The toddler is constantly on the move during this period; he bangs things around and is very disrupting. This child hears "no, no," so much he may think his name is "no, no." At two or two and a half, the youngster wants to be demanding and dictatorial. He is truly a "little stinker." He throws a tantrum if he does not get his way. He balks at new things. He often wants to hear the same stories over and over and over.

Management of the child can be difficult at this time, unless the parents repeatedly apply patient, loving guidance, and discipline. Much space and discussion will be spent on this very important age, for it is in this early time that parents are laying the foundation for a life. It has been said by many educators that the first five years of a child's life are vitally important. There is much for the parent to do during this crucial phase of development. The correct handling of the child and the problems that arise now can make a great deal of difference in the child's life and development in the years ahead.

There are many who think that the child should have the run of the house. Coffee tables should be cleared and lamps placed out of reach. It is my opinion that breakable objects should *not* be removed; everything should stay in its place. The young child should be taught that he must leave some things alone. In fact, if you allow your child freedom to touch and pick up breakable objects at home, then he certainly will do the same thing away from home. Love your child enough to spank his hands when he reaches for objects he should not have, and he will be a welcome guest in other homes. Otherwise, your friends and neighbors will wish you had left the "little stinker" at home.

Now what do you do if your two-year-old throws a temper tantrum? One young fellow of two decided he would have his way or else. The lad flopped down on the floor, kicked his feet, and screamed. The child's very wise and loving mother showed no surprise. She merely turned out the light, stepped over the child, and left him to scream. As mother listened, the child's cries grew fainter. Soon her two-year-old son joined her in the living room. You see, tantrums are used to get attention. The boy received no attention; he found out his antics would not work. He never had another one.

Some parents are terrified by the child who, when in a rage, cries so hard that he holds his breath. The parents are afraid to walk off and leave the child for fear that he will not breathe. The parents pick him up, console him and usually let him have his way rather than discipline him as they should. A spanking might bring on more crying and another breath-holding episode. Don't be intimidated. The child should be ignored, and he will stop crying. If the child should hold his breath long enough to pass out (this rarely happens), he will automatically start breathing on his own.

NEVER ASK "DICTATORS" FOR A DICISION

Because the two-year-old is dictatorial, never ask for a decision. Approach every encounter with a positive instead of a negative attitude. Say, "Let's pick up the toys," and then see that the toys are in place before the child hurries on to some other activity. If any activity that the child undertakes is done wrong, encourage him immediately to do it correctly. For example, if the youngster decides to write on one of his books, give him paper to write on and say, "It's so much more fun to do things the right way." Make "the right way" more fun by rewarding him with due praise and compliments.

The one and a half to two and a half-year-old child may decide not to eat correctly. If he chooses not to eat at meal time, serve him small portions, and leave the food on his plate without comment. When the meal is over, compliment the child if he has eaten well. If he did not choose to eat, say nothing, but give the youngster absolutely nothing to eat (allow water only) until the next regular mealtime. Do not fret! Your child will not starve; in fact, he will eat what his body needs. Above all do not let this little angel of yours get the "best of you." Be firm!

WHATSOEVER THINGS ARE TRUE, HONEST, ETC.

Since this is a fast learning age, fill your child's head with good notions, good ideas. Your child is learning how to talk so do not let him pick up slovenly habits. I personally believe in teaching the toddler to have respect for adults by saying, "yes, ma'am" and "no, ma'am" "yes, sir" and "no, sir."* Such replies are far more mannerly than a grunt of "yeah" and "nope." Teach your child to call adults Mr. and Mrs. (last name) and that first names are to be saved for children his own age. Do not think this is too much to expect of a child who is just beginning to talk. If mother is on the job, it is easy for a child to learn manners at this age that can (and will) be carried on through life.

I know all this works, because that is the way I trained my own children. I now have a two-year-old grandson who says to his nursery teachers on Sunday Morning, "Thank you, Mrs. Richardson," "Thank you, Mrs. Gilkey." He has an extensive vocabulary for a two-year-old that includes "yes, ma'am," "no, ma'am," "thank you" and "please."

*I realize that in some parts of the country, families are much less formal, and in some cases parents would feel uncomfortable with having their children say, "yes, sir" and "no, ma'am." I still strongly believe in teaching children to have respect for elders. How you do it is up to you; just be sure to work on *doing it*.

Yes, it all took much practice and repetition on the part of his parents, but such teaching will pay big dividends. My grandson has learned early what many children do not learn until they are grown. In fact, some children never learn *any* manners. And *it does make a difference.*

START SPIRITUAL TRAINING EARLY

This age, one and a half to two and a half, is the perfect time to teach the child love for the Lord. The child's head will be filled with something, so fill it full of things worthwhile. Give your child a small Bible of his own, and tell your child Bible stories. Teach your youngster scriptures and help him memorize them. Teach your child to sing praises unto the Lord now. Impossible? No, it is not.

At this writing my wife and I are the grandparents of three youngsters—a three-year-old granddaughter, and two grandsons, ages two and one. All three of these children are hearing Bible stories daily. Children love to be read to and if they are not, they are being deprived of great joy. So, we and their parents believe that they should hear the stories of God's love for His children, and His children's love for Him. It is not too early to tell the story of salvation in words that even a two-year-old can understand.

You ask the question, "Teach a two-year-old to memorize scripture?" If you love your child and want your child to love the Lord from his earliest years, it can be done. Just this summer our two-year-old grandson came for a visit. Since his grandmother did not want to send him to the church nursery for Vacation Bible School, she decided to have Vacation Bible School at home. Every morning John Mark heard a Bible story, and learned a simple scripture verse. Of course, the scripture verse was learned with repetition as grandson and grandmother played during the day and as he said his prayer at night. But the lad was learning something worthwhile and felt like a "big boy" because he, too, had gone to Vacation Bible School.

Also, teach them to sing. This past summer, John Mark, at two, and his sister, Rebecca, at three, learned to sing the books of the New Testament. In fact, Rebecca had her first opportunity to use a talent for the Lord as her pastor let her sing "The Books of the New Testament" for an evening service.

Also teach the child choruses that he can sing by memory. As I was traveling with John Mark the other day, I found that he knew some thirty-five to forty choruses, such as "For God So Loved the World," "The Wise Man Built His House Upon a Rock," "Safe Am I," etc.

These children will never remember the day when they were not singing praises to the Lord and memorizing portions of His Word. There may be skeptics here and there who say, "Poor darlings, those children are being pushed too hard." We pay no attention to such criticism. We did the same thing with our own children, and now that they are grown with children of their own, we are glad to see the cycle being repeated.

A sense of humor helps get the parents through the one and a half to two and a half year stage, but if necessary use firm discipline to keep the youngster in line. If he is allowed to do as he pleases at this age, the parents are in for permanent behavior problems in the future.

Remember that mother and father should

be working together and enjoying each phase of their child's development. Mother and father are sharing in the care of the infant and at the same time enjoying each other. By their mutual love and affection, mother and father give the child a sense of security and teach him love by example. *Secure happy parents have secure happy children.*

4

Childhood:
A Time of Change

The period of growth and development from two to twelve years is usually called the childhood stage. It is a time of constant change, constant learning, and almost constant movement (motion). In order to do the right kind of job for children during this period, the parents must be energetic, alert, and dedicated to the task of parenthood. This period shows why the Lord gives children to young people—older parents can seldom keep up the pace necessary to do the best for their growing children.

TERRIBLE TWO BECOMES HAPPY THREE

The "terrible, dictatorial" two-year-old soon reverts to the pleasant, happy child of three. The three-year-old is a pleasure to have around and the only problem is that he is sometimes awkward. The three-year-old tends to fall and may whine and whimper because it makes him feel insecure. All this child needs is love, attention and sympathy.

FOURS CAN BE FEARSOME

Soon the child reaches the age of four and he is suddenly "out of bounds in all directions." This age youngster tends to be difficult and boastful. Fiction seems much more interesting than fact, so the child may tell all sorts of interesting stories and call them the truth. At this age, the child may bite people (children or adults), hit people, and throw rocks; he may even run away from his parents.

The four-year-old may shock mother by suddenly letting out profane words. Hopefully these words were learned at the neighbor's house and not at home. Remember that children learn by watching and listening to adults. Never say things before your children that you do not want them to say or repeat. This applies to bad language, opinions about friends and neighbors, or just family affairs that do not need repeating in front of company.

Parents should be careful of the correct usage of grammar, because the children will imitate them in speech and in action. Parents must set the right example, because children attempt to be like parents. If parents are critical of everything and everybody, the child learns to condemn; if parents are fearful, the child learns to be apprehensive and unsure of himself. Remember that through parents' speech, dress, and behavior the parent is teaching the child.

The four-year-old's problems must be met with firm discipline. Set limits and stick to them. If the child learns that mother and dad mean business and that when they say "no" they mean "no," problems are avoided or quickly corrected.

FIVE—THE CALM BEFORE THE STORM

The five-year-old seldom presents many problems and is easy to get along with. However, this pleasant age does not last. The child suddenly becomes six years of age and enters into a stormy period of development.

SIX—OFTEN "AT WAR" WITH EVERYONE

The six-year-old is very emotional and seems to be in rather constant conflict with everyone. The child now is very rigid and demanding and seems to be making a drive for independence. The six-year-old may cheat, steal, and accuse others of doing these things. Of course, parents should have already taught the child not to take things that belong to others, but if the child does steal something from a neighbor or from a store, he should be immediately corrected and made to return the stolen property.

A young woman who is a patient of mine

admits that even though she is now an adult and the mother of three children, she will never forget the correction her father gave her for stealing. At an early age she secretly slipped something home from a store. Her father discovered what his daughter had done, and he carefully pointed out her error to her. The father then sat down with his daughter and his Bible and read aloud every scripture that had the vaguest reference to "Thou shalt not steal."

The father then *went with* his daughter to the store where she had taken the merchandise, made her return the article, and apologize to the cashier. The young woman remembers her humiliation until this day, and, needless to say, she was completely cured of taking something that did not belong to her.

The six-year-old may suddenly tell her mother, "I hate you," or "I'll kill you." A few minutes later she will say, "I love you." These fluctuations in the child's response show the emotional conflict that is characteristic of this age.

One reason for problems at six is that children start to school. This is always a tremendous adjustment, and some children, especially boys, may not be ready for school. By this time you should know if your child is ready for school. Some children do not mature as fast as others, so, if the child is not ready for school, it is much better to keep the child home an extra year. It is much better to start the child to school a year later and have him confident and at ease than to start him too soon and have him insecure and poorly adjusted. Occasionally a child will be promoted through the first and second grades and have a difficult time "keeping up." If this happens, it is wise to let the child repeat a grade in order to let him "catch up" and enjoy his schoolwork in future years.

One of my young patients was a girl who cried and did not want to go to school each morning. The girl would cling to her mother and say her tummy hurt. This went on for several weeks and usually the mother would force her daughter to go on to school. Occasionally, however, she would let the child stay at home with her grandmother. Examination revealed no physical health problems, so I talked to the child's teacher. The teacher explained that the youngster was timid and would not join in class activities, although she did play well at recess.

Another interesting feature of this case was that the youngster enjoyed Sunday School. The child apparently enjoyed Sunday School because she did not have to learn on a competitive basis. The teacher, mother, and I agreed that the child was too immature for the first grade, so she was allowed to wait another year before starting school.

Starting to school can be a problem if the parents have not prepared the child properly. The child should be taught and guided in such a way that he is anxiously awaiting the opportunity to enter school. Parents should assist and encourage the child with every problem and with school work, but at the same time insist on discipline. The child who has never been disciplined at home encounters his first real problem when he enters school and the teacher insists on having her way. Other children also insist on their rights and the child is amazed because this new world does not say "yes" to his every whim as mother and dad have always done.

Parents must begin in the first grade to share an interest in the child's schoolwork. When the child arrives home from school, mother should meet him, if possible, and inquire about the activities of the day. If mother is genuinely interested, the child will grow up wanting to share his activities with mother and dad. The child will always feel free to come home and share the many things that he had encountered. This communication will give the parents the opportunity to discuss, praise, correct, and guide the child through many situations. In the same way the parent must examine the schoolwork, praise the child's accomplishments, and know that the youngster is getting his schoolwork done.

Parents should help the child read, write, and develop the many skills that are presented at school. Our teachers can only do so much, and they do not have the necessary time to spend with each student to develop his talents. If someone at home does not teach and encourage the child, he may be a mediocre student all his life. Even at this age the child should be taught that he is expected to do the very best that he can in every activity that he undertakes. It has been proved that even a child will try to live up to what is expected of him. If you expect mediocrity, you get mediocrity.

SEVENS CAN BE VERY IMAGINATIVE

The seven-year-old has usually made the adjustment to school and is much easier to live with. This age child may want to be alone more, is very imaginative, and tells some very hard to believe stories. Remember that imagination is a wonderful characteristic, but help the child realize that you know the difference between imagination and fact.

The parents of the seven-year-old will be plagued with the child's desire to watch T.V. In fact, this age child will stay "glued to the set" if the parents do not set some guidelines. Rules as to when, how much, and what the child watches must be made by the parent and these rules must be firmly adhered to.

At our home we set a rule that the T.V. set would not be turned on from Sunday night until Friday night unless a teacher had insisted that the student watch an educational program. The rule that was made for the children was strictly followed by the parents, also. There was no static from anyone concerning T.V., for it simply did not exist in our minds until Friday night. Then if something "watchable" was on the schedule, T.V. was something special for the family to enjoy. Randall, our seven-year-old, thought T.V. on Saturday morning was a special treat.

EIGHT IS OFTEN IN A HURRY

By eight years of age the youngster is happy, enthusiastic, and cocky. This age child is in such a hurry, he pays little attention to manners or cleanliness. It is not unusual to find the eight-year-old gulping his food and talking with his mouth full. But be sure that the table manners you and your child started when he was two years of age are still followed.

You may have to slow your eight-year-old down in order to have him remember to do some necessary things. Very early one Saturday morning our youngest son, Randall, was in a tremendous hurry to get to baseball practice. Randall ate breakfast hurriedly and with just enough manners to "get by" his mother. He left the table with a muttered,

"Excuse me," ran to his room, picked up his baseball cap and glove, and ran back through the dining room hoping to dash out the back door. Just as Randall tried to bolt past his mother in the dining room, she stopped him and asked if he had brushed his teeth. Randall's reply was, "Mother, why should I brush my teeth? They'll just get dusty." Needless to say, that young, "in a hurry" fellow hurried right on to that early morning ball practice *without* brushing his teeth.

The eight-year-old thinks he can do anything. He starts many projects eagerly but rarely completes them, because his interest span is rather short. This age child may be upset by failures but starts something new immediately. He is best managed by encouragement and trying to protect him from doing too much.

NINE STARTS REACHING OUT

The nine-year-old, for the time, shows more interest in friends and outside activities than in his family. It is essential that the parents guide the child in selecting both his friends and his activities away from home. Your child should play with children whose parents are the kind of people you approve of and who are teaching their children properly. The child learns many things from his playmates, so you certainly want him with children who will be a good influence instead of a bad influence. You do not want your child at someone's home if the parents in that home are doing things that you do not approve. Of course, you can't put your child in a glass bubble. He will come in contact with all types of children from all types of homes. Teach him to be friendly, nice, and play with these children, as long as they are doing things that are right. But the children that he spends much time with should be carefully selected.

Nine-year-olds also need guidance in choosing activities. By this age children are engaged in baseball, swimming, music, plus activities at school and church. Music lessons should have been started by this time, and the child should be encouraged in any field of endeavor for which he shows a talent. A common problem is too many opportunities. Children don't have enough time to engage in all the good and worthy choices, and be careful that he does not substitute the "good" for the best.

Remember to always show a genuine interest in your child's activities. This applies to the three-year-old's discovery of a bug just as much as it does to the nine-year-old's Little League baseball efforts or the teenager's football or basketball games. Your interest causes your child to enjoy his activities more and to be anxious to come to you to share his experiences. Many teaching opportunities arise as your child dicusses joys and problems that arise from day to day.

Along with parents' interest must go teaching and encouragement. If parents teach the child that only his best is expected in any endeavor, the child will usually put forth that effort. Praise the child, win or lose, for doing his best. Remember to give praise for a job well done. Constructive criticism is important, but always be sure to give praise along with pointing out mistakes.

A young woman I know recalls how, at a very early age, she learned from her father that as a Christian she was to live each day to the fullest. This young lady remembers that her dad never sat around and waited for good things to happen; her dad *made* them happen by plain hard work. This very wise father taught his daughter in early childhood to work as hard as she could and then to be happy with the outcome. This girl learned a valuable lesson early, and this knowledge has helped her have a happy life thus far.

RESPECT FOR AUTHORITY MUST START EARLY

Remember, as time goes by, the parents should be the first authorities to be respected by the child. This respect for parents' authority must be taught by patience and firm discipline. If the parents are firm and consistent in the rules they make and are consistent in enforcing these rules, the child will obey and learn respect for authority.

The child should learn early that violating the rules of those in authority results in punishment. The young child should also be shown that obeying the rules results in benefits to him and not just to those who make the rules. If this point is firmly established, the child will grow up appreciating rules and laws as something set up to benefit rather than as something set up to limit his freedom or to punish him.

The nine-year-old tends to be independent. He becomes an expert at exploiting adults and uses one parent to outdo the other. The nine-year-old also begins to worry about his school activities, and if he is not doing well, he may pretend to be sick to avoid going to school. The child usually complains of stomachache or headache. These symptoms are difficult to evaluate, but unless the child has fever, vomiting or diarrhea, he can usually be encouraged and sent to school. It helps to treat the nine-year-old as if he were older. If the parents are supervising his schoolwork as they should be and helping when necessary, then problems seldom exist.

Of course, children *can* get sick, so if the child complains of stomachache too often, get a medical opinion. Children can have "nervous indigestion" with abdominal pains based on anxiety or tension, and the child may need medication for relief. Be reasonable but firm.

Make school attendance important—a "must" unless something is really wrong. Then your youngster will not "play sick" in order to stay home and avoid some unpleasant situation at school.

TEN—THE "NICE" AGE

The ten-year-old is suddenly the nicest person around. He actually tries to be good! This child considers his parents the final authority and wants to obey them. A child this age especially wants to spend time with his father. Fathers, no matter how busy you may be, you should manage to be with your child *now* instead of putting him off until he is older and "more interesting." If you have little time for your child now, when he is older, he will have little time for you.

Wise parents will enjoy watching and encouraging their children together. At this age, Little League baseball plays an important part in many a child's life. Some parents refuse to watch their children perform in sports and other activities due to several, I feel, mistaken ideas. One mother insisted that it made her daughter nervous, and the girl did not perform as well if mother was watching. This to me shows a faulty relationship and would be true only if mother were overly critical of the young lady's efforts. If parents encourage, praise, and require only that the children do their best, then most youngsters *want* their parents present and will do their best at that time.

Another reason parents give for not watching their children perform is that they know nothing about the activity. This is certainly a poor reason. The rules of any sport can be learned by a little reading, listening, and watching. My wife had never seen a basketball game until our first son started playing. My wife soon became an enthusiastic and knowledgeable basketball fan. If parents are interested in their children, parents will watch the children in their activities as much as possible.

That children truly appreciate parents' interest in their activities is illustrated by the following excerpt from a college theme that was shared with me by my daughter, Marsha.

"An outstanding characteristic of my

parents that has had tremendous influence on me is that they made my interests their interests. They have turned down many invitations in order to encourage me in my endeavors. Even though my parents' interests did not always coincide with mine, they have always been by my side to support me. For example, my mother is as unathletic as a person can be and cares very little for sports. However, since I was a participant, she became an ardent fan of basketball and tennis. She had never seen a game until her children started playing basketball in the sixth grade, and she never missed a game during the next seven years.

"Dad never missed a complete game. When he was not there, I knew a patient needed him. Occasionally, the fans were not very courteous, but I could remain composed, for I knew that there were two people in the stands who were on my side.

"Another example of this unusual interest is that dad never missed coming with mother to a piano recital. Many of my friends' fathers did not attend, but I could depend on my dad to be there. For twelve years my piano recitals were of vital concern to him."

Parents, your presence and interest *does* make a difference!

ELEVEN—OFTEN OBNOXIOUS

The eleven-year-old is rude, blames others, holds grudges and demands extra privileges. This age youngster gets along poorly with brother and sister and is generally obnoxious around the home. He likes to raid the refrigerator, but has little use for soap and water. Girls at this age are beginning to be aware of their breast development and may be embarrassed. This age is best managed by making fewer demands, but being firm.

TWELVE—LOVES EVERYTHING

The twelve-year-old has become enthusiastic again and "loves everything." A youngster this age does a great deal of day dreaming but likes to arrange his own activities. The girls are becoming very interested in boys, but, generally, they still have little use for the girls. The girls are maturing rapidly. Girls at twelve may begin menstruation, breast enlargement, and show other signs of growing up. At this stage the earlier maturity of the girls is most obvious. The boys do not really become interested in girls for another year or two.

During this twelve year period boys and girls may seek *more* sex information. I use the word *more*, for the mother has by now answered in a perfectly natural way, the normal questions pertaining to sex that her boy or girl has asked as they have developed through these first twelve years. Interestingly enough, if the channels of communication have been kept open, the twelve-year-old boy will rely on his mother for answers to his questions about sex. It behooves mother to be prepared with the correct answers, so that her son (or daughter) will not have to rely on misinformation from his friends. According to some teachers of this age group if boys and girls have not been taught at home, they will spend much time in the library seeking information from dictionaries and books.

The young girl must be prepared for the onset of menstruation well in advance to avoid a reaction of fear and shame when she does begin to have her menstrual periods. The girl should be taught early that as a preparation for eventual motherhood, she will have a monthly "period," which is a normal vaginal bleeding. If the girl realizes that this "bleeding" has a purpose and is very normal, she will look forward to the beginning of her "periods" as a sign of growing up.

5

The Teen-age Years

This period of development, is the time in a young person's life that most parents dread. It is during these years that many children become independent and rebel against their parents. They may become defiant and get into all sorts of trouble. It is at this stage that many parents "give up" and let the youngster do as he pleases. This usually means that the teen-ager does many things that often ruin his or her life physically, emotionally, or both. Even the teen-ager who "survives" doing as he pleases, often looks back on these years with deep shame and regret and blames his parents for not remaining firm in their discipline and helping him avoid these mistakes.

Since this is such an important time in the young person's life, the teen-age years will be discussed in this chapter year by year; in the next chapter, teen-age problems.

The thirteen-year-old becomes moody and withdrawn. This new teen-ager may lock himself in his room and stay away from the family. The problem is that the thirteen-year-old is maturing enough to worry about things.

He is now concerned with popularity, school achievement- - -and money.

The boy at thirteen has never before realized that money can be a problem. He has always had what he needed given to him by his parents. Spending money has usually been provided automatically. Now he thinks of more expensive items that he may want, he suddenly finds that dad's money is not unlimited; the family money has to be spread out to cover many needs.

Girls at thirteen become very critical of home, but never criticize home to other people. She may complain that mother is old-fashioned, that mother does not dress fashionably, and that mother does not understand a young girl's problems. However, in these early teens she usually tells people outside her family how wonderful her parents are.

The answer to this stage is reassurance. Let your thirteen year old think. Let him try to figure out all his newly discovered problems. Always respect his closed door. However, always know up to a point what is going on behind that door.

I know one mother who insists that it is only good manners to knock before entering when a door is closed. When her children were all at home, this mother insisted that each person in the family would respect the other enough to "knock before entering." However, she still made it a point to know what was going on behind the closed door. From time to time she would knock ever so gently and take the "closed in" child a coke, cookies, or some other goody. This wise mother knew what was going on, just as she knew that her child needed some time to be alone.

FOURTEEN IS USUALLY FRIENDLY

As age fourteen is attained most young-sters are happy and joyous. The fourteen-year-old is usually very friendly and likes to talk things over. When a youngster of any age wants to talk, the parents must take time to listen. If this policy is continued throughout the child's life, he will always feel free to discuss things with his parents and many problems will be avoided. If the parents are perceptive and available, they might receive the compliment that one mother received from her daughter, who wrote: "Then there is that almost undefin-able person, my mother. It is hard to find adequate words to describe her. She is loving, kind, unselfish, and understanding. She is a good listener, a good companion and friend. She has laughed with me, cried with me, and has given up many things in her own life for me."

The fourteen-year-old likes cars, records, clothes and seems to live on the telephone. Rules concerning the time to be spent on the phone are practically a must; in some cases a second phone line for the family is a good investment. The second phone can backfire, however, as it did when one youngster always used the family phone to place calls. That way his line was always open in case another friend called him! Parents, it is up to you to make rules concerning the use of the telephone and follow through on the rules you make.

The fourteen-year-old is concerned about clothes. But parents should not make the mistake that one young girl's parents made. Their teen-age daughter was putting far too much emphasis on dress. The mother and daughter were spending a great portion of dad's monthly check on clothes for the daughter, because the popular young lady insisted that she simply had to have a new dress for every Friday night ball game!

Young people should be aware of the family finances. The young person should be taught early in life to have some regard for the needs of other members of the family. This is certainly applied to material possessions.

Some young people today, (yes, even at fourteen) say that parents have put too much emphasis on material possessions. I heard such "words of wisdom" come from one fourteen-year-old as she was sitting on the floor surrounded by her record player and an endless array of records.

Parents, teach the child early that it is not so much what you have that matters; it is what you *are* that really counts.

As fourteen-year-olds participate in sports and academic endeavors, it is important to place less emphasis on winning, or being first. Instead, stress sportsmanship along with the physical and mental training that will help the young person in later years. Certainly all of us like to win, and every parent wants his child to be good enough in his chosen activities to win. Inevitably, however, someone must lose. This striving to win but learning to lose is the important matter. Note that I say "learning to lose." Some people have a harder time learning how to win. Parents must teach the child how to do both.

A winner should be happy, pleased with himself, and yet humble. No one appreciates a "big headed," boastful winner. A loser, provided he has done the very best he could do at that time, should be satisfied and determined to try even harder the next time. Players who show anger and misbehave during competitive activity are hurting themselves as well as their team and their sport.

Teach your children to win or lose with a smile. Yes, it is disappointing to lose, especially in a closely fought contest, but as long as one has done his best, losing is no cause for tears or temper tantrums. Losing should make one evaluate his performance and then do what is necessary to improve— more study, more practice, more rest, more concentration.

In my time I have played in many a tennis match, and I have also watched many matches. I still have a hard time respecting even the best tennis player when he (or she) throws the racket and has the temper tantrums of a two-year-old.

As I taught my three children to play tennis, we made the rule that temper or disgust even at oneself was not to be displayed on the court. Each child knew never to drop or throw his racquet in disgust (after all you only have to go retrieve it). Our children lost some, and won some, but it was required that they show good manners and sportsmanship or they would be removed from the court, not by the rules of the Texas

Tennis Association but by the rules they and their parents had made together. Young people prefer to behave correctly; they only need someone to help them.

FIFTEEN BECOMES MIXED UP, SULLEN

Suddenly the joyous, friendly fourteen-year-old becomes a fifteen-year-old mixed-up adolescent. The fifteen-year-old is restless and sullen. This teen-ager wants to be up late and to be out of the house as much as possible. This is the age when the child is farthest from his parents. Girls are especially interested in necking, and some boys enjoy this entertainment, too. However, the boys are also concerned about jobs and their futures. This unhappy age must be met with patient, loving guidance, and firm but fair discipline at every turn.

Since the fifteen-year-old is striving to be as far away from his parents as he can be, he may enter the house and go directly to his room. This "retreating" is fine, if he retreats in a proper manner.

One young man of fifteen arrived home from school in a rather unsettled state of mind. As he entered the house, he slammed the door with such force that the house shook. His mother, who was standing in the kitchen waiting for a greeting, was rather appalled at this behavior. As he stormed on through the house to his room with not so much as a "hello," his mother stopped him. She insisted that he return, open and close the door properly, and greet his mother in the manner he had been taught. The young man learned in a hurry that being "mad at the world" was no excuse for disgusting behavior toward those who loved him.

SIXTEEN—SWEET, HAPPY FRIENDLY

Usually, the sixteen-year-old is "sweet sixteen," happy and friendly again. At this age the teen-ager returns to his parents and wonders how mother and dad learned so much since last year. Problems arise but are handled in a much more mature way.

The sixteen-year-old is the "bud" stage of

maturity that one hopes will continue to develop into the full "rose" of maturity by the age of twenty-one. Some people are mature by age twenty-one; some do not mature until the age thirty or forty.

The seventeen to eighteen year olds are exposed to more problems outside the home—problems at school and problems in dealing with their associates. If parents have done a good job up to this stage, the parents will be able to reassure and counsel the young person as he applies the knowledge and standards that the parents have taught him. He will turn to his parents for the advice and reassurance he needs as he progresses toward individual maturity.

The eighteen and nineteen-year-old has a much "looked forward to" experience as he leaves home for work or college. For the first time in his life, he is actually "on his own" without close parental supervision. He is now exposed to the realities of the world— many of which are not good. The temptations and opportunities to do any and everything wrong is almost overwhelming. However, if parents have accomplished the goal of instilling Christian standards, this maturing teenager will be happy and on his way to making a success of his life. If the young person does not have high ideals and goals, he may easily plunge into every evil and unwholesome activity that is presented to him. Of course, this path leads to unhappiness and perhaps destruction.

6

Problems of the Teen-age Years

During teen-age years few families escape at least some problems. If the parents have done the job they should have up to the teen years, and *do not quit*, most problems are easily handled. Unfortunately, many parents who have apparently done a good job of guiding the child up to this stage now lose complete control. There are several reasons for this, but a major cause is that parents go soft, or try to "be more reasonable" with their fast developing young person.

Teen-agers will test their parents in many

situations. If the parents stand firm in what they have taught all along, the young person will be satisfied; but if the parents give in on some points of their teaching, the teen-ager will push more and more to go along with the crowd. By now the young person should have such a good background of teaching that all he needs is a reminder and encouragement to help him "stand his ground."

TEEN-AGER'S DECISIONS SHOULD COME FROM WITHIN

Remember that throughout the child's life you have been teaching him *why* he has been told to do things or not to do things. If you have led the young person to understand why and have convinced him that your reasons are correct, then he will be prepared to make decisions based on what he knows is right or wrong, instead of decisions based on his parents' demands. In fact, the indication of maturity that all parents strive for is to have their youngsters make proper decisions on their own.

Throughout the teen-age years, parents must continue to discuss all problems, answer all questions, and listen to their youngster's wishes and ideas. If the young person's ideas are acceptable, by all means, follow them; if not, try to convince him *why* his suggestion is not best. If he will not agree, then the parents must demand that he follow their wishes as long as he is a member of their household.

Remember that this decision-making is a lifelong training process. When your child was small, you let him make decisions that really did not matter. For example, you asked, "Will you play with your train or your ball?" Soon you progressed to, "Will you wear your red shirt or your white shirt?" (not "Will you wear your shirt or go naked?").

As a child matures, parents should let him make the decisions he is capable of making correctly. If he makes the wrong decision, stop him immediately, and use this as a teaching opportunity so that when this situation arises again, he will make the correct decision based on his own knowledge and beliefs.

One young co-ed at Hardin-Simmons

University refused to attend Sunday School and church with the other girls in her dormitory. Her father is a Baptist preacher. The girl's excuse was, "I went to Sunday School and church every Sunday all of my life. I even played the piano for every church service the last few years, so I'm tired of *having* to go to church." This girl and her parents had certainly "missed the boat." The preacher father was so busy with other people that he failed to instill in his daughter a love for God. Long before college age, this young lady should have been going to church because it was God's house, and because she loved God, not because her dad happened to be the pastor and made her go.

Do not let children, young or old, make decisions you know are wrong. That is what parents are for—to prevent children from having to make all the mistakes the parents made in order to learn. You certainly would not let a toddler decide to play with fire or drink something that might be poisonous. Then do not let a teen-ager make the wrong decisions about wearing bikinis and dresses that are entirely too short, about going to evil places of amusement, about participating in worldly activities, or keeping company with questionable companions. Some wrong decisions in these areas could harm their lives as much as the fire or poison could have harmed them when they were very young.

YOU ARE IN CHARGE, NOT YOUR TEEN-AGER

Parents, do not be guilty of sitting back and saying, "I wish my child wouldn't do so and so." Remember that *you* are supposed to be in command and not the child. Just as parents are supposed to set the infant's schedule and not let the infant set their schedule, so they are to see to it that the teen-ager does as he has been taught.

Do not give up just because you are facing a teen-ager.

Whether it is a matter of picking up scattered belongings, getting home from a date on time, wearing longer skirts or shorter hair, the family teaching must be enforced. As the teen-ager proves to his parents that he is mature enough to make wise decisions, then he automatically gets more and more freedom that leads to adult responsibilities.

The so-called "generation gap" is really a lack-of-communication and discipline gap. This gap will not exist if the parents have maintained discipline all along and have established a relationship with their children that encourages discussion of all problems.

The main problem during the teen-age years is that the youngster is neither child nor adult. The teen-ager wants the privileges of both stages of development but does not want the responsibilities of either. The teen-ager wants money without working, he wants to set his own schedule without regard for others in the home, and wants unlimited freedom without the responsibilities that freedom involves.

POPULARITY CAN HAVE A HIGH PRICE

During the teen-age years, group pressures are very influential. The youngster wants to be one of the gang, to be popular. The young person must be taught that real success is being different from the crowd. Anyone who just follows along doing what the crowd suggests will never be anything but a follower. To be a success, one must be willing to do what he knows he was put here to do, what he thinks is best. He must refuse to do what he knows is wrong or questionable, no matter who suggests the course of action.

Of course, everyone needs and wants friends, but this is accomplished by being kind and friendly and not by trying to please the gang or follow the "hero" of the hour. Always remember, "You can please all of the people some of the time, and some of the people all of the time, but you cannot please all of the people all of the time." Anyway, if you try to please everybody, you will never please yourself.

Unfortunately, many parents encourage their children to do "anything" to be popular. Mothers especially have a tendency to push their daughters (and sons) into dating, partying, and other activities long before they are really ready. The important thing is to develop personal standards and try to have a few genuine friends who will try to live by Christian principles instead of trying to be popular with the masses.

When I think of teen-age parties and young people with established convictions, I remember a particular instance that happened to a young teen-age boy not too many years ago. The young man was invited to a party that was being given in his neighborhood. His parents checked on the type of party being planned. Then they decided with their son that he could go.

When he returned home from the party, the boy told his parents all that had occurred. It seems that plans for some of the games were changed and apparently he had not been a very cooperative guest.

The daughter for whom the party was given suggested the game of "Post Office" or "Spin the Bottle." The group sat in a circle with a bottle in the middle. One was chosen to spin the bottle, and the one the bottle stopped on would have to take a walk and kiss the "spinner."

The grandson in question was rather disgusted by the proceedings, because he insisted that when he wanted to kiss a girl, he would kiss one of his own choosing. Since he was not "in" on the game, he chose the only empty room in the house, the bathroom, and sat in there and *enjoyed* looking at the

Montgomery Ward catalog. Square? Perhaps some would say, "yes," but this young man had been taught to save his affections and love for the "right" person at the right time.

RULES HELP TEEN-AGERS BUCK THE CROWD

During these trying years, it is a tremendous help to the young person for the parents to make rules and enforce them. This helps to overcome some of the group pressures. Rules are needed concerning study hours, frequency of dates, outside activities, proper hours to be home after activities, etc. Young people appreciate rules, although they may complain about them. They can "save face" with the group, if necessary, by quoting the rules and blaming their course of action on their parents.

Young people will use mother and dad as an "out," if mother and dad have taught them correctly. For instance, one afternoon a mother was waiting for her daughter after school. When the bell rang, the daughter rushed up to the car and said hurriedly but quietly, "Mother, say I can't go."

Shortly one of her classmates came to ask the mother if the daughter could go to a party. It was a party that the daughter really did not think she should attend, but she hated to refuse the invitation, so she relied upon her mother to help her out of a sticky situation.

As the teen-ager becomes more mature and more independent, he will just say, "I don't want to do that" or "I don't believe in that." Until he gets to that point, rules definitely help the young person as he gropes his way to maturity.

EVERYBODY ELSE IS NOT ALWAYS DOING IT

In some situations, especially in small towns or in a local area, group rules are helpful. Parents can get together and set rules for the entire group. This prevents the argument that "everyone else is doing it," and saves a great deal of discussion in many homes.

The question, "Why can't I go? Everybody else is going," is heard many times from the teen-ager. In the first place this is an inaccurate statement, for "everybody" else could not possibly be going. However, teen-agers possess an unusual amount of persistence, so the young person may continue to plead.

In one such case a young man desperately wanted to go to a movie on a school night. The teen-ager knew that his family's rule was that he did not attend movies on school nights. For some reason, the boy especially wanted to go on this particular evening. The only "valid" reason the boy would give his mother was, "Everybody else is going."

The mother finally gave in to his pleadings with the remark, "Son, I guess it'll be fine for you to go to the movie. I'll take you down there, but you'd better be sure that 'everybody else' will be there." The mother left the discussion with those words.

An hour or so later the son came in to tell his mother that he had decided that he did not want to go; he had more interesting things to do. I have a suspicion that the boy knew full well that "everybody was not going." Parents should not fall for this time-worn phrase.

WHAT TO DO WITH REBELLION

What should parents do if they try to be patient and loving but in spite of all their efforts their youngster rebels and refuses to cooperate? All support, financial and emotional, should be withdrawn. Very few rebellious young people would remain rebellious if their parents did not continue to pay their bills. Many members of the recent "hippie" movement received regular checks from home. It was easy for these young people to "fight the establishment" and accuse parents of being too money-conscious as long as they received money without having to earn it.

Fortunately, most young people survive their teen-age years; somehow, their parents do, too. Eventually teen-agers mature into young adults who are willing to assume responsibilities and contribute to the world in which they live. Some parents of teen-agers may have their moments of doubt and despair; they may be ready to give up. At times like that they must take a new grip on their convictions and reach deep down inside for a little more grit, and a lot more trust in the Lord for strength and wisdom.

Hebrews 11:1 has special meaning for the parents of a teen-ager: "What is faith? It is the confident assurance that something we want is going to happen. It is the certainty that what we hope for is waiting for us, even though we cannot see it up ahead" (TLB).

7

Choosing A Mate:
Life's Second Most
Important Decision

As parents teach their children, trying to help them attain the goal of a full and happy life as a mature adult, there are many, many attributes that must be instilled in their lives—honesty, love, respect for the rights of others, and discipline. As they develop and mature most young people are beginning to think about finding a husband or wife with whom they will share the remainder of their lives. This is a vital step in the lives of your children. Getting the right partner helps insure a life of happiness. Getting the wrong partner can mean a life of misery and failure.

If we as parents have shown a proper love and the right kind of affection for each other and for the children, then the children will be prepared to find a wife or husband and start their own home properly. Over the years parents should take the opportunity to point out examples of happy homes and of unhappy homes and why they are that way. Unfortunately, it is all too easy to show them examples of broken homes that have resulted from alcohol, unfaithfulness, indifference, immaturity, etc. It is too easy to show them young people who are pregnant before they are married, who are living in such a way that they have no respect for each other or for themselves.

THE BEST STANDARD IS THE BIBLE

Parents must teach their children the truths that are taught by the Bible. Throughout history these truths have been proven over and over. As people ignore Biblical truths, they ruin their lives.

One of the foremost teachings in the Bible concerning marriage is that one man and one woman unite to form a permanent family. The two are to love each other as they love themselves and become one in their mutual love. Jesus taught, "Have you not read, that He who created them from the beginning made them male and female, and said, 'for this cause a man shall leave his father and mother, and shall cleave to his wife; and the two shall become one flesh'? Consequently they are no more two, but one flesh. What therefore God has joined together, let no man separate" (Matt. 19:4-6, NASB).

All this "free love" one hears advocated today sounds wonderful except for two things: it is *not free* and it is *not love*. "Free love" can cost a person his or her self-respect, hope for happiness and often health. The immorality advocated in our times as "free love" has led to a tremendous increase in out-of-wedlock pregnancies, venereal disease, drug addiction, suicides, and mental illness. Participation in this style of living makes it impossible for an individual to ever enjoy a marriage, because marriage as established by God calls for mutual love and trust. True love is based on sharing and caring so much that the two become as one. Such a relationship cannot occur between more than one man and one woman. The sexual "freedom" advocated today by many people reduces man to the animal level of lust in which no love, consideration or respect is involved.

Our children should be taught that true love grows out of a friendship based on mutual interest and admiration. The long period of growing up and meeting many people of the opposite sex should be a time of enjoyment. A young person needs to be around *many* others to find that *one* person suited for him or her for life. If parents have succeeded in establishing the goals of education and maturing before marriage, the children will not be in any hurry to get married.

BE CHOOSY WHEN SEEKING A MATE

In our society today many girls, as well as their parents, are frantic if they are not engaged by high school graduation or, at the latest, by college graduation. This frantic fear that they will not get a husband causes many girls to settle for someone they know is not what they really want. This results in many unhappy marriages that end in divorce.

It all reminds me of the joke about the hunter who said, "I'll kill the first animal that jumps out of the brush for my supper." And the first one that jumped was a skunk! The point is obvious: DON'T BE DETERMINED TO MARRY THE FIRST PERSON WHO IS AVAILABLE!

The Christian young person especially should never hurry in selecting a mate. God has a plan for each life and will lead him or her to the right lifetime partner.

Young people should enjoy dating others without getting too serious, until they are sure that the right person has come along. Each person should save his love and deep affection for that special someone. It is sickening to see some of our young people putting their hands all over each other. It is a disgusting sight to see young people necking and petting in cars, in the halls at school, on the school grounds, etc. The worse thing is that this undue affection is shown to any boy or girl who is available at the moment. This often leads to sexual involvement, which has no place outside of marriage.

In deciding who might make a good partner for life, there are many things to consider. It is important to take plenty of time and become well acquainted enough to know as much as possible about the person. Infatuation and physical attraction are a poor basis for a lifelong relationship. Even couples who have known each other for a long time find characteristics showing up after marriage that they did not expect. Marriage following a short acquaintance is, more often than not, headed for trouble.

CHRISTIANS SHOULD MARRY CHRISTIANS

Sharing mutual interests and spending time together talking and sharing experiences will help one find the right partner. If a boy and girl have similar ideas and beliefs, they will be happier together. Religious background and practices are of extreme importance. A Christian can never be truly happy if he is married to a non-Christian, and those who marry in the belief that they can win their mate to Christ after marriage are most often doomed to failure.

If a couple cannot agree on a religious faith before marriage, they should not get together. When two very different religions are involved the marriage has more problems. If each remains faithful to his or her religion, it means separation of the couple for many hours, which would be spent together in a religiously united home.

When children come along even more problems arise. No couple going to different churches can do as good a job as parents as if they were together. Remember we discussed the necessity of parents "sticking together" in teaching and leading the growing child. Parents who are split on religion or on church affiliation present a confusing picture to the growing child. Most of the children in such a home end up with no religious convictions, and without this important ingredient in their lives, they are seldom truly happy.

SIMILAR EDUCATION LEVEL
IMPORTANT

In looking for a mate, it is important to have similar education levels. When one member of a family has much less education than the other, it is difficult to have similar interests. Too many times a wife will work and support the family while the husband finishes his education, only to have him lose interest and leave her, because she is not his intellectual equal. This is another reason why parents should emphasize to the children all their lives that marriage is for adults, and that marriage follows the attainment of their education goals.

It is important to spend enough time with the person you are considering as your lifetime partner. Be sure you can be happy with his or her habits. Anything that you do not like should be discussed and settled *before* marriage. Do not plan to change your mate *after* marriage. Certainly both partners will make some changes in their lives, but habits, especially bad ones, are seldom changed. Someone who drinks alcohol will probably continue to drink. Someone who smokes will probably continue to smoke. Someone who likes to hunt and fish and live outdoors will be miserable if his partner tries to make him stay inside and do things he is not interested in.

A speaker I heard at a Bible conference put it well when he said, "If a bus has Cincinnati on the front, don't get on that bus hoping to talk the driver into taking you to Dallas. It is not about to change its destination."

Maturity is important in a marriage partner. No matter how carefully one selects a wife or husband many problems will arise. If both partners are mature, they can work out the difficulties. If one partner is immature, he or she is usually selfish and unwilling to work to solve problems. If both partners are immature, the situation is even worse. This is the reason that so many "teen-age" marriages fail. These young people should still be at home being guided by their parents toward maturity instead of trying to establish a home of their own. Marriage is definitely for adults only!

8

"Ye Shall Reap
What You Sow"

The greatest joy a parent can have is to see his children grown, happy, and successful. I hope through these pages that you have learned additional ways to attain this joy. Many hours—even years—of persistence and hard work are necessary to guide your children along the way, but all the time and effort are worthwhile when you can look around and say, "I have raised these children and am proud that they are my own."

In Galations 6:7 we read: "Be not deceived; God is not mocked: for whatsoever a man soweth, that shall he also reap" (KJV). This scripture is never more true than in this matter of rearing children. Those who ignore their children and simply let them grow up, those who set poor examples for their children to follow, and even those who give in and let their children make mistakes which they could have prevented will probably reap a harvest of unhappy, unsuccessful children. Watching them make a failure of their marriages, a failure of their careers, and usually a failure of rearing their own children is a tragic experience. These parents are forced to make excuses for their children and are often reluctant to even admit whose children they are.

The parents who have "sown" properly are rewarded by seeing their children form happy homes and make a success of their chosen careers. They watch their children enjoy the time and effort that is necessary to help rear the next generation of children toward the goal of maturity.

"And let us not be weary in well doing: for in due season we shall reap, if we faint not." (Galations 6:9, KJV). The parents who realize the individuality and value of each child, who strive to rear the child to be the best person he can be spiritually, physically, mentally, and emotionally—will have a lifetime job—a job dedicated to giving to the next generation someone worthwhile. But parents, that is why we are here. How glorious it is to do the job of rearing children well! When the job is well done, you can reap the benefit of "a peace that passeth all understanding" and perhaps, just perhaps, your children may rise up and call you "blessed."

NOTES:

NOTES:

NOTES:

NOTES:

NOTES: